JUNIOR MARTIAL ARTS
Confidence

Junior Martial Arts

ALL AROUND GOOD HABITS

CONCENTRATION

CONFIDENCE

HAND-EYE COORDINATION

HANDLING PEER PRESSURE

SAFETY

SELF-DEFENSE

SELF-DISCIPLINE

SELF-ESTEEM

Junior Martial Arts
Confidence

Kim Etingoff

Mason Crest

Mason Crest
450 Parkway Drive, Suite D
Broomall, PA 19008
www.masoncrest.com

Printed and bound in the United States of America.

First printing
9 8 7 6 5 4 3 2 1

Series ISBN: 978-1-4222-2731-2
ISBN: 978-1-4222-2734-3
ebook ISBN: 978-1-4222-9067-5

The Library of Congress has cataloged the
    hardcopy format(s) as follows:

Library of Congress Cataloging-in-Publication Data

Etingoff, Kim.
  Confidence / Kim Etingoff.
    pages cm. – (Junior martial arts)
    ISBN 978-1-4222-2734-3 (hardcover) – ISBN 978-1-4222-2731-2 (series) – ISBN 978-1-4222-9067-5 (ebook)
  1. Martial arts–Juvenile literature. 2. Self-confidence–Juvenile literature. I. Title.
  GV1101.35.E785 2014
  796.8–dc23
                         2013004748

Publisher's notes:
The websites mentioned in this book were active at the time of publication. The publisher is not responsible for websites that have changed their addresses or discontinued operation since the date of publication. The publisher will review and update the website addresses each time the book is reprinted.

Contents

1

MORE THAN FIGHTING

What do you think about when you think of martial arts? Do you think of punches and kicks? Do you think about being strong?

People who **practice** martial arts know how to punch and kick. They know how to knock down opponents. But they also have a particular way of thinking. They're in control of their bodies. They're also in control of their minds.

Millions of people practice all kinds of martial arts around the world. And millions more know what martial arts are. They've seen actors use martial arts in the movies. Or they have friends who study martial arts.

In karate, students learn groups of moves called kata. Students have to learn each move and perform them in the right order.

But what people might not know is that martial arts are about more than just fighting. They're about getting better as a person.

There are lots of reasons martial arts are good for you. They teach you **self-defense**. They help you to stay healthy. They show you how to focus. Martial arts teach you to respect other people. Martial arts can change the way you think about yourself and others.

Kinds of Martial Arts

Martial arts are all ways to teach people self-defense. There are many different kinds of martial arts. Each kind of martial art is different.

Some martial arts started in Asia. Karate is one of the most famous kinds of martial arts. Karate is from Japan. It comes from older Chinese martial arts and also from Okinawa, an island in Japan. The karate we know today was created in the 1900s.

In karate, students stand up. They don't usually use any weapons (or fake weapons). There are a lot of punches and kicks in karate, using hands, elbows, feet, and knees.

CONFIDENCE

Taekwondo comes from Korea. It means "the way of the foot and fist." Taekwondo was first taught in the 1950s, but its roots come from older Korean martial arts.

Students of taekwondo move their feet and legs a lot. They learn how to kick and throw down opponents.

Capoeira is another kind of martial art. It's from Brazil. We don't know exactly how it started. But we do know that African slaves in Brazil started capoeira a few hundred years ago.

Capoeira is practiced as a game. In the game, two people fight each other. There is music, and people sing and play instruments. It's like a mix of dancing and fighting.

These are just three examples of martial arts. There are many, many more. Some are practiced mostly standing up. Some focus on throwing people to the ground. Some use your legs more, and some use your arms. There's a martial art out there for everyone!

Skills for Success

A lot of martial arts are about self-defense. If you ever really needed to, you could fight off someone who was attacking you.

But that doesn't really happen much. Most martial arts teach you much more than how to fight someone trying to hurt you.

Martial arts teach you how to relax. You learn to focus on getting better at something. You learn new things, like balance and **hand-eye coordination**, from martial arts. You learn to respect other people.

You can use all the things you learn in martial arts in your life every day. If you get better at focusing on things, you'll do better on tests and homework. Then you'll get better grades and learn more.

Getting better at balancing can help you in lots of ways. You can use your new **skills** in any sports you play. Better balance can help you in dance.

All About Confidence

One important thing you learn from martial arts is confidence. Confidence is belief in yourself. If you have self-confidence, you think you can do things well. You trust yourself. When you're confident, you feel good about yourself.

It can take a lot of time to learn any kind of martial art. Students don't start off breaking boards in half. But over time, students learn more and more. Soon, they can reach goals like breaking boards or earning new belts.

Let's imagine you have to give a presentation in class. You have to stand up in front of everyone and tell them about something you did.

If you don't have a lot of confidence, you might be very nervous. You might think you won't do well. You won't be able to talk about your work. You might

CONFIDENCE

worry that everyone will think you're boring. You might be afraid of getting a bad grade.

If you are confident, you think differently. You might still be nervous, but you'll know you can do it. You'll be proud of the work you did. You'll believe that you can talk about it to your whole class. If you're confident, you can deal with feeling nervous.

When you give the presentation and you're not self-confident, you might look nervous and worried. You won't speak up. You'll rush through your report or get stuck.

But when you give the presentation with a lot of confidence, it shows. You speak up. You tell the class what they need to know. And you get a good grade!

Confidence isn't something that we're all born with. It's true that some people have more confidence than others. But we can all learn to be more confident. Learning martial arts is one way that we can build more confidence.

Taekwondo Goals

Learning taekwondo can build up your confidence. In taekwondo, your teacher will help you set goals. When you meet those goals, you'll feel proud! Your confidence will go up. At first, your goals might be really small. If you're just starting, your goal might be to get a walking stance down right. That's one of the first things you start learning. As you get better, your teacher will help you figure out bigger goals. Doing a simple kick perfectly might be a good goal. When you get really good, your goals will be bigger. After a while, you might want to try kicks while jumping in the air! Making and meeting goals is a great way to build confidence with martial arts.

CONFIDENCE & MARTIAL ARTS

P racticing martial arts is one of the best ways to learn more confidence. But what does confidence have to do with learning how to roll and kick?

Hard Work

Martial arts are hard! Most people can't just watch the teacher and learn a new move right away. They have to practice and practice before they can get it right.

If you stick with it, you'll see how much better you get at your martial art. At first, you won't know what you're doing. You might feel clumsy. You may not remember the order of the moves.

After practice, you'll start to get better. Your teacher might give you some tips. You'll start to remember how to do the new moves. Slowly, you'll see you've learned your new move!

When you do things well, you can't help feeling good about yourself. At first, you couldn't do the move. Now you can. It was a **challenge**. But you did it. You know that you can do hard things. You feel better about what your body can do.

Moving Up

In most martial arts, like karate and taekwondo, you move up levels as you get better. You start out at the beginning. You have to work hard and pass some tests to move up. If you stick with your martial art for a long time, you'll reach the top.

The good thing about martial arts is that you're only **competing** with yourself. You challenge yourself to get better. When you get better at a certain move or learn something new, you feel proud.

You don't have to compare yourself to other people. If someone else in class moves up a level and you don't, it's okay. It doesn't matter because you're not competing with that person. Nothing bad happens to you when she moves up.

Moving Up in Karate

In karate, your belt color tells you what level you're at. As you move up, you might feel better and better about yourself. Different kinds of karate have different colors of belts at each level. When you first start out, you might have a white belt. As you get better, you move up to yellow. Next, you move to a gold or orange belt. After that, you can move to a green, blue, and purple belt. The next step is brown or red. Some of these might be switched around in your karate school. The last belt is the black belt. You have to practice karate for years to get a black belt. And even then you can keep getting better. After you get a black belt, you can move up the next step in the black belt. There are ten steps in all to get to the very top.

Getting a new belt can help you to feel good about your hard work. It can help you feel confident!

CONFIDENCE

Students earn different colored belts in karate, taekwondo, judo, and other martial arts. Earning a new belt can make you feel confident. You did the work to move up a level and you've got the belt to prove it!

Having confidence means not worrying about what others are doing. Instead, you focus on how you can make yourself better. You'll move up when you're ready. Pretty soon you'll see how much better you've gotten since you started.

Competition

Some people like to compete. They like a challenge. For those people, competing with others can build confidence.

In most martial arts, you have the chance to compete with other people. Some martial arts, like judo, are very competitive.

If you know you're going to compete, you'll practice a lot. You want to get as good as you can to beat the other person.

You have to be careful when you're competing against others. Losing can make you feel bad. It can make you feel worse about yourself and how hard you work. But losing a competition doesn't have to hurt your confidence. Losing doesn't mean you can't ever win. You can always get better. Losing can push you to practice more and get even better.

And if you win, you'll feel great! You'll know that you can do something well. It's a big boost to your confidence.

Don't let it go to your head, though. Just because you won a competition, doesn't mean you can stop working hard. There are more competitions to win in the future. Confident people can feel good about themselves, win or lose.

Class Time

It's hard being a kid sometimes. You might get picked on. You might have trouble getting good grades. There might be times you feel left out. All of that can make you feel bad about yourself.

Martial arts teachers know that. They know everyone has trouble being confident. So they make martial arts all about teaching confidence.

In every class, you'll hear that you can do things. Teachers know that everyone in class can get better. They **encourage** people. They want everyone to keep trying. Encouraging words from your teacher can help keep you going.

You'll hear a lot of encouraging words during a martial arts class. Everyone wants you to do well. You'll hear things like, "You can do it." Or, "Not being perfect is okay, just keep trying." Or even, "You've gotten a lot better!"

Hearing these sorts of things can help a lot. You'll start to feel good about how much you've learned. And you'll start to feel confident about the new things you can do. Encouragement can help build your confidence.

Standing Up for Yourself

Lots of kids are picked on at school or online. It makes kids feel bad. If someone tells you you're dumb or ugly, you can't help but wonder if they're right.

Martial arts can give you confidence to stand up to bullies. But that doesn't mean fighting back or hurting others. Martial arts are just as much about knowing that you don't need to fight. Martial arts teach you how to not let bullies make you feel bad about yourself. You don't want to fight a bully, even if you do know martial arts. First, it's not a good way to solve any problem. Second, you can get in big trouble. Remember, martial arts are about more than fighting. They're about having the confidence *not* to fight.

Martial arts can help you seem more confident to everyone around you. You'll stand up straighter. You'll look people in the eye. Bullies don't want to pick on people who are confident.

Martial arts also teach you to not listen to what bullies say. If someone calls you lazy, for example, you know that's not true. You know that you work hard at martial arts. And you're getting better all the time!

Confidence in Martial Arts

At first, martial arts help you have more confidence. After that, it works the other way. Your new confidence helps you get better at martial arts.

After a few weeks or months or years doing martial arts, you know what's going on. You know how classes work. You know your teacher. You know that you've gotten better and learned a lot.

You're probably not as scared or nervous anymore. You have more confidence about what you can do in martial arts.

Of course, you're still learning. You can always learn new things in martial arts. And now you have the confidence to learn the hard things.

By now, you won't just give up because something is hard. Maybe you're trying to learn a harder move. You've never done it before. You might even fall down the first few times you try.

You could just give up. Someone without much confidence might give up. He would think he couldn't do it.

But you won't give up. You know you've figured out how to do hard moves before. Some took you a really long time. In the end, though, you learned them. Now you do them all the time.

So you keep practicing. You're confident that you can do the move with practice. You practice and practice. Slowly, you figure it out. In a few weeks, you know the move well. You can do it again and again with no trouble. And all because you had the confidence to keep trying!

3

BUILDING YOUR CONFIDENCE

Most of us could use some help learning to be more confident. Sometimes we're not very confident about anything we do. We feel like we won't be good at anything we try.

Some of us are confident about doing some things, but not others. If you're really good at drawing, you might be confident about that. But you might not feel as confident about math class. Maybe you have trouble in math class, and you don't like it at all. Maybe you're really good at sports, so you feel confident when you play on teams. But you might also feel less confident about playing music. You may stay away from trying to play instruments.

When we become more confident, we try to do more. We can understand math better and get better grades. We can try playing instruments. Confidence helps us try things that might have seemed scary or hard before.

Martial arts can teach you a lot about sticking to something even when it's hard. When you get knocked down in martial arts, you have to get back up and try again. You won't win every competition, but you can try your best and learn more each time.

But there's no magic way to gain more confidence. We have to work at it. Luckily, there are some things we can do to become more confident.

Think Positively!

There are lots of things we can do to help ourselves. The way we think has a lot to do with whether we're confident or not.

If you're trying out a new move in a martial arts class, you can think about it two ways. You can tell yourself it's too hard. You might think it will take a really long time to learn. You can think that everyone else will get it before you do. All these thoughts are **negative**.

Negative thinking won't get you very far. Thinking negatively is like fighting yourself. Negative thoughts won't help you in martial arts. They won't help you do other things well, either. Negative thoughts can keep you from doing well on homework, studying for tests, or in sports.

Positive thoughts will help you much more than negative ones. When you're learning that new move, think, "I can do this." You might know that it will take a while to learn the move. You'll also know that if other people can do it, you can too. Think about how good it will feel when you do the new move perfectly.

Those are positive thoughts. Thinking positively helps you do big things. Positive thoughts help you gain confidence. If you're always putting yourself down, you won't have any confidence. If you cheer yourself on, you'll feel good about yourself and what you can do.

Thinking positively can be hard work. If you catch yourself thinking negatively, stop! Try to turn your thoughts around. Once you get used to positive thoughts, it will become normal to think them all the time.

Challenge Yourself

A lot of us are afraid of challenging ourselves. We're afraid we might not do well. We stick to doing things we know we're good at or that we're comfortable doing.

But it's good to challenge yourself. You never know what sort of things you might be good at. And you'll never know until you try!

You could choose to try martial arts. Or you could start learning how to play the guitar. Or you could join the student council. There are lots of choices.

You might not be perfect at those things when you first start. That's okay. It's not often someone is great the first time she tries something.

If you stick with what you choose to try, you'll get better. You'll see that you can do something new. And you'll feel really good about yourself. That's how confidence grows. By never trying anything new, you won't give yourself a chance to get more confident.

Music and martial arts might seem very different. But both take practice and mean performing in front of others. Performing in front of people can be scary, but it's also a great way to build confidence.

Acting, Music, and More

Performing arts are a good way to challenge yourself and become more self-confident. Acting, dancing, or playing in a band or orchestra are all performing arts.

Think about acting. You get to pretend to be someone else. You might feel better about talking to other people. Or standing up in front of an audience.

Once you know you can do something like that, you get more confidence. If you can talk to people you don't know on a stage, you can do it in real life too.

Performing arts can be hard. But with practice, you can become a better dancer or actor. When you practice an instrument and get better, you feel proud and happy.

You can use the confidence you gain through dancing or art or music in the rest of your life. You might feel more confident that you'll do well in school. Or that your friends like you. Confidence helps you every day.

Building Confidence in Martial Arts

Of course, martial arts also help you build confidence. You can practice your confidence at the same time you're practicing your kicks and throws.

You can practice thinking positively. Every time you come across something you can't do, don't get angry. Imagine yourself doing that step in a few weeks. You just have to practice. After some time and hard work, you'll have much less trouble than when you started.

Martial arts are full of all sorts of challenges. There are always new things to learn and ways to get better. And there are also lots of ways to boost your self-confidence once you learn all those new things.

Set goals for yourself. Talk to your teacher to figure out what goals good are for you. It could be a big goal like getting to the next belt level in karate. Or they could be smaller goals, like getting better at doing one move.

Challenge yourself to pay more attention to the teacher. Make a friend in class. Remember a move you learned months ago. There are all sorts of goals you can set in martial arts.

Practice is always important in reaching goals. You won't get there right away. Let yourself make mistakes. Ask for help. Watch your teacher or other students.

When you reach your goal, you'll be proud of yourself. You trusted yourself to get better at martial arts, and you did! That's what confidence is all about.

At the Top

Even the best martial artists have had to build up their confidence. British Paralympic judo champion Ian Rose used to not have much confidence. (The Paralympics are like the Olympics for disabled athletes.) Ian is partially blind. When he was little, other kids used to tease him. He felt like he couldn't fit in because of his blindness. Then he started judo. He says, "After four months, I was a different person. Judo rebuilt my confidence." He realized he was really good at judo. And he ended up winning lots of championships and medals!

CONFIDENCE & YOUR LIFE

C onfidence is important. Inside and outside of martial arts, feeling good about yourself can make your life better. Believing in yourself can help you in lots of ways.

In School

Doing well in school has a lot to do with confidence. Getting good grades and speaking in front of your class are a lot easier when you believe in yourself.

Not having any confidence in school won't help you at all. Without much confidence, you might worry about not doing well on your next test. You might believe you're going to get a bad grade. That's not the right **attitude**!

If you're more confident, you'll know that you have what it takes to do well. You'll study, because you'll believe you can do well by working hard. You can go into the test with a good attitude. You can hold on to positive thoughts.

School is for learning. Having a hard time can be a big part of learning. You don't have to do well all the time. Everyone has had trouble at some point. What's important is learning from your mistakes and going on. When you're confident, you don't let your mistakes get in the way.

When you feel good about yourself, you can do more and more. Because you feel good about what you can learn, you try to take harder classes. You learn more and you find new things that you like to learn about. If you don't have the confidence to try new, harder things, you'll never know what's out there!

Friends

Being confident helps you with other people, too. When you're confident around your friends, you'll have a better time.

Imagine that your friends all want to go ice skating. You've never done it before. You're afraid to try it because you think you'll be bad at it. You aren't confident that you can ice skate.

You start asking your friends about ice skating. You find out that two of your friends that are going have never ice skated either. But they're excited to try something new.

You get excited too. You're still a little nervous, but you think you'll have a good time. And you do! You fall down a few times, but your friends who have skated before help you out. After a little practice, you can skate around by yourself. Now you know you like skating. You might even want to take skating lessons.

This is a good example of changing negative thoughts to good thoughts! At first, you weren't very confident. But then you chose to challenge yourself. You had fun. You learned new things. And you ended up gaining confidence because you found out that you could skate.

Your friends will be happier if you're confident. You'll be willing to try new things. And maybe your own confidence will push them to be confident too.

No one likes to be teased or bullied. Good friends won't make fun of you or make you feel bad about yourself. Confidence comes from inside, but if your friends are making you feel bad, it might be time to look for new friends.

Feeling Good About Yourself

Confidence is something every kid should have. We should all feel good about who we are and what we can do. Sure, there are some things that you probably won't be able to do really well. But there are plenty of things that you can do well. Focus on those, and you'll gain confidence before you know it.

No one wants to feel bad about themselves. We want to feel proud of what we can do. We want to be able to try new things.

Martial arts are one of the best ways you can gain some confidence. Whether you're practicing capoeira, fencing, jiu-jitsu, or taekwondo, you'll learn confidence. Then the confidence you learn in martial arts will become part of the rest of your life!

A Big Problem

Bullies are a big problem. If you've ever been bullied, you're like a lot of other kids. The United States Department of Education says that about one out of every four students have been bullied in school. One out of every sixteen kids is bullied every single day. Being bullied makes life hard and not very fun. By building your confidence, you can stand up to bullies and not let them bother you.

Some karate schools have special classes about standing up to bullies. Classes will teach you how to stay away from bullies. They teach how to look and feel confident. They teach you about dealing with your problems without fighting. Lots of kids who take karate want to stand up to bullies. These classes can help them do it!

Words to Know:

attitude: How you show how you're feeling about what you're doing and the people around you.

challenge: Something difficult you have to work hard to overcome.

competing: Going against at least one other person in a sport or activity to see who wins.

encourage: To share kind words that help others push themselves to do their best.

hand-eye coordination: How well your eyes, mind, and hands work together to do things like catch a ball or use a pencil.

negative: Having to do with something that makes you feel bad.

positive: Having to do with something that makes you feel good.

practice: To learn, use, and train to become better at something.

self-defense: Stopping another person from hurting you and making sure you're safe from danger.

skills: Things you learn that help you become a better person or live a better life.

Find Out More

Online

All Star Activities
www.allstaractivities.com/sports/karate/Karate-belt-system.htm

Kids Web Japan: Judo
web-japan.org/kidsweb/virtual/judo/index.html

PBS Kids
pbskids.org/itsmylife/body/solosports/article2.html

In Books

Iedwab, Claudio. *The Peaceful Way: A Children's Guide to the Traditions of the Martial Arts*. Rochester, Ver.: Destiny Books, 2001.

Peterson, Susan Lynn. *Legends of the Martial Arts Masters*. North Clarendon, Ver.: Tuttle Publishing, 2003.

Scandiffio, Laura. *The Martial Arts Book*. Toronto, Ont.: Annick Press, 2010.

Index

About the Author

Kim Etingoff lives in Boston, Massachusetts, spending part of her time working on farms. Kim writes educational books for young people on topics including health, nutrition, and more.

Picture Credits